# Coxcomb
## *Variations*

*Anita Shackelford*

**American Quilter's Society**
P. O. Box 3290 • Paducah, KY 42002-3290

Located in Paducah, Kentucky, the American Quilter's Society (AQS) is dedicated to promoting the accomplishments of today's quilters. Through its publications and events, AQS strives to honor today's quiltmakers and their work and to inspire future creativity and innovation in quiltmaking.

EDITOR: Bonnie K. Browning
BOOK DESIGN/ILLUSTRATIONS: Jarrett Sims
COVER DESIGN: Michael Buckingham
PHOTOGRAPHY: Charles R. Lynch, except where noted


**Library of Congress Cataloging-in-Publication Data**

Shackelford, Anita.
Coxcomb variations : AQS legacy collection / Anita Shackelford;
American Quilter's Society.
p. cm.
ISBN 1-57443-747-X
1. Appliqué--Patterns. 2. Patchwork--Patterns. 3. Quilting--Patterns.
I. American Quilter's Society. II. Title.
TT779.S425 2000
746.46'041--dc21

00-010422
CIP


Additional copies of this book may be ordered from the American Quilter's Society, PO Box 3290, Paducah, KY 42002-3290 @ $18.95.
Visit us on the web @ http://www.AQSquilt.com

# Contents

# The Quiltmakers

*Mary Clark*

*Sharon Finton*

*Darlene Garstecki*

*Carol French Grossman*

*Janet Hamilton*

*Sheila Kennedy*

*Jo Lischynski*

*Erena Rieflin*

*Connie St. Clair*

*Judy Spence*

*Anita Shackelford*

# *Introduction*

Using an antique quilt for inspiration is an easy way to begin to design new work. The quilts in this book were made as the result of a challenge posed to a group of friends. Every quilt was made using the same basic set of templates, which had been traced from a nineteenth century coxcomb appliqué quilt.

The challenge of creating original work was new to many of the quilt-makers participating in this project. The templates gave us all a place to begin; from there, creativity blossomed. Everyone who worked on this challenge enjoyed it immensely. There was excitement each time we shared ideas, studied fabric selections, and looked at color drawings or mock-ups. We found that we were able to create an amazing variety of designs by simply changing the color selection and the arrangement of the pieces. Some of the quilts include slight variations in the shape of the original templates, one uses the templates in a smaller scale, and three quiltmakers added other motifs to the designs of their quilts. Look for the distinctive design elements detailed for each quilt.

Twelve new quilts are pictured, along with the templates and fabric requirements to make each one. I hope they will inspire you to create your own coxcomb quilt.

A complete set of patterns for the original quilt is provided on pages 10–15. In the variations, pattern pieces are provided only when there are changes from the original patterns.

# The Original

## Original Coxcomb

Antique coxcomb, mid-nineteenth century, unknown quilter, Ohio or Indiana

# Original Coxcomb

The original coxcomb quilt was purchased at an estate auction in my hometown of Bucyrus, Ohio. I have always been interested in antique appliqué quilts, and I love the bold look of these coxcomb arrangements. The large, somewhat primitive, appliqué is a style that I associate with the German women who made quilts in Pennsylvania, Ohio, and Indiana in the mid-nineteenth century.

The background quilting patterns are another feature that attracted me to the original quilt. Quilting in the ditch surrounds each appliqué piece, but instead of the more usual lines or grid, the background is filled with charming "cookie cutter" shapes which include hearts, leaves, flowers, ovals, diamonds, and other interesting little designs. There is no quilting within the appliqué pieces.

The workmanship on the original quilt is not fine and much of the appliqué has changed color. Leaves that I assume were originally green are now a medium tan. Other small pieces have lost their color completely. Even though the quilt was not in perfect condition, I decided that the unusual pattern outweighed the flaws. Little did I know when I decided to bid on this quilt where it would eventually lead.

## Distinctive Design Elements

Cookie cutter quilting designs & reverse appliqué details

# The Reproduction

## Coxcomb with Birds

Hand appliquéd and hand quilted by the author, 1995

# Coxcomb with Birds

Being first and foremost a quiltmaker, my immediate thought was to re-create the antique quilt in what I imagined had been strong red, green, and orange – colors so often found in mid-nineteenth century appliqué quilts from Pennsylvania and Ohio. Templates were made by tracing the motifs directly from the quilt. Many of the shapes were irregular and were not necessarily the same from block to block. I took them as they were, feeling that the irregularities were part of the charm of the quilt.

*Artist's statement –*

For the appliqué fabrics, I chose a solid red, a dark green with a fine black print, a strong orange for the accent color, and muslin for the background. It was exciting to see the design begin to develop in these bold colors. I kept the size of the background blocks and the templates as close as possible to the original quilt. The edges were finished with a piped binding.

| | |
|---|---|
| Quilt size | 84" x 84" |
| Center block | 36" x 36" |
| Side blocks | 24" x 36" |
| Corner blocks | 24" x 24" |

## Yardage

3 yds. Red solid
3 yds. Green print
⅓ yd. Orange solid
5 yds. Muslin (background)

# Distinctive Design Elements

Orange accent color, blanket stitching

## Quilting Design

Lines of quilting surround each appliqué in the ditch and ¼" beyond. The background is filled with cookie cutter shapes traced from the original quilt, plus some of my own design.

# Patterns

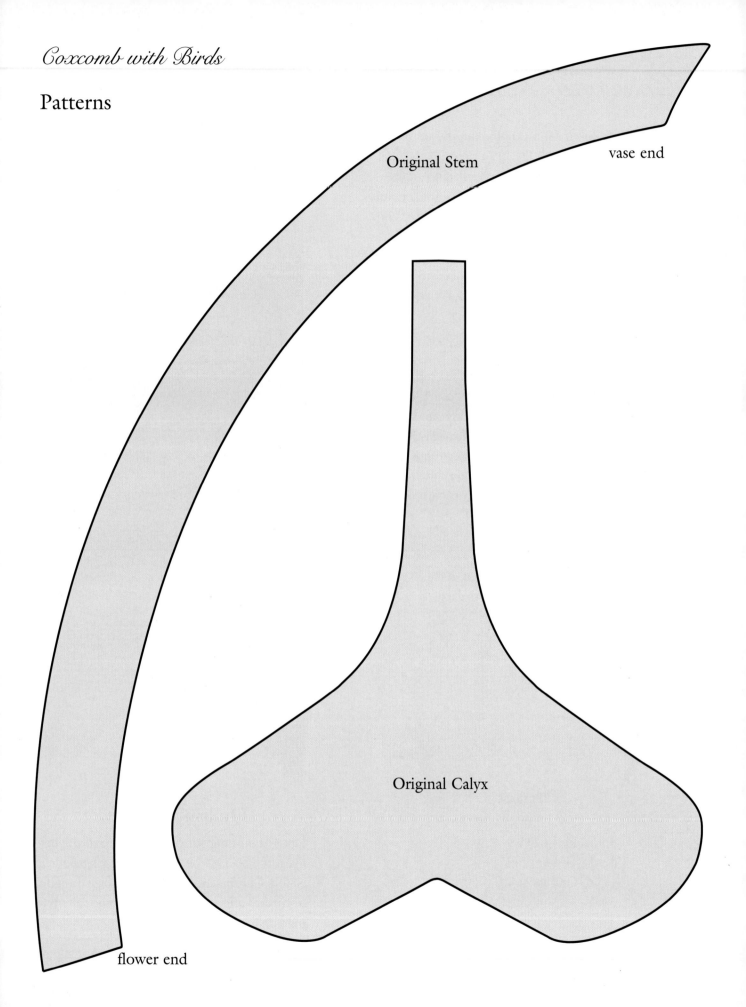

Original Stem

vase end

Original Calyx

flower end

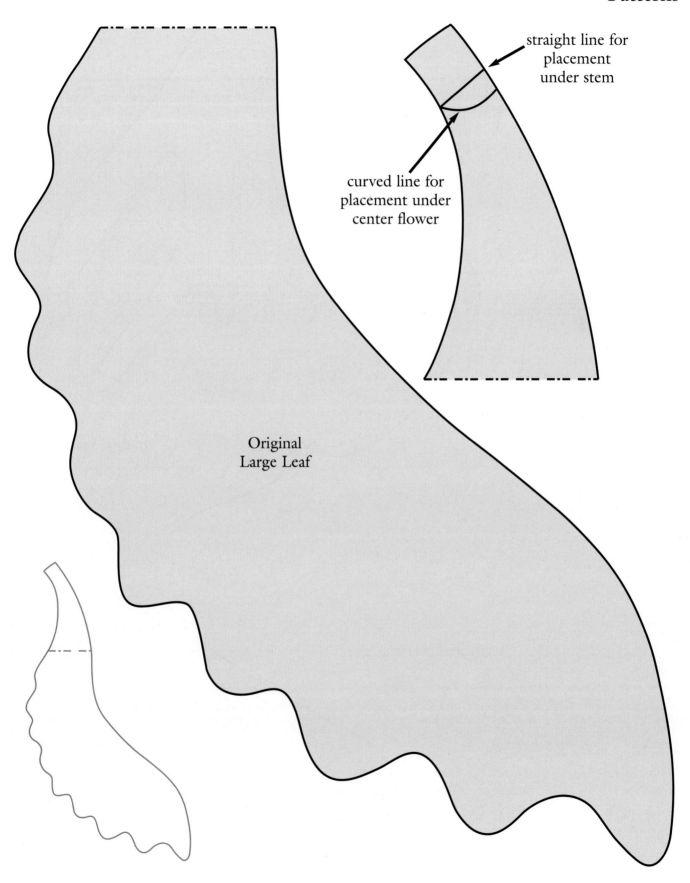

straight line for
placement
under stem

curved line for
placement under
center flower

Original
Large Leaf

# Patterns

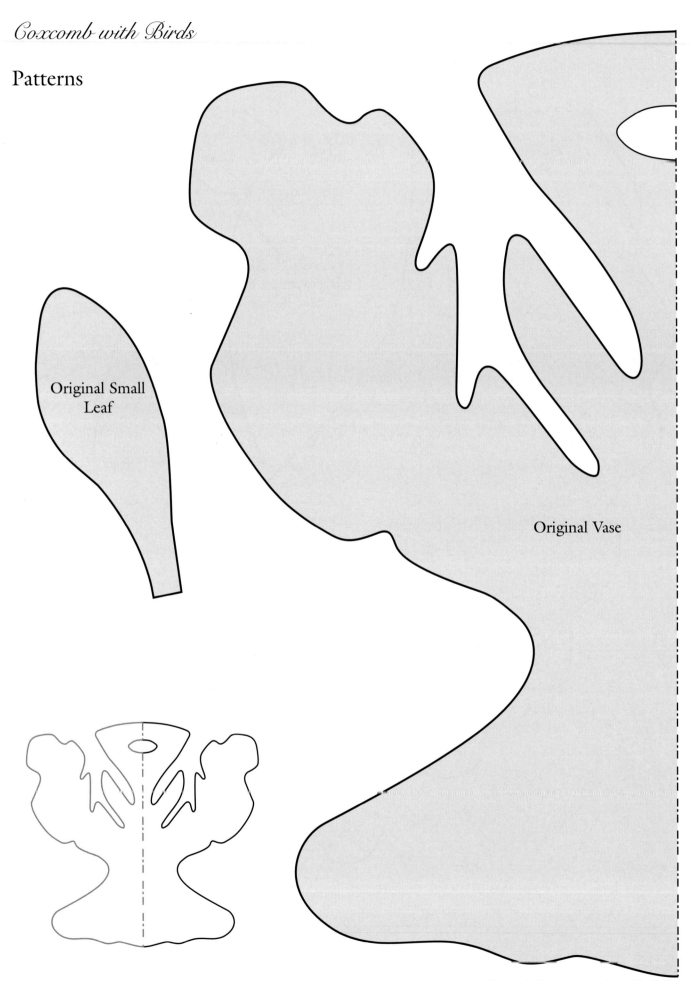

Original Small
Leaf

Original Vase

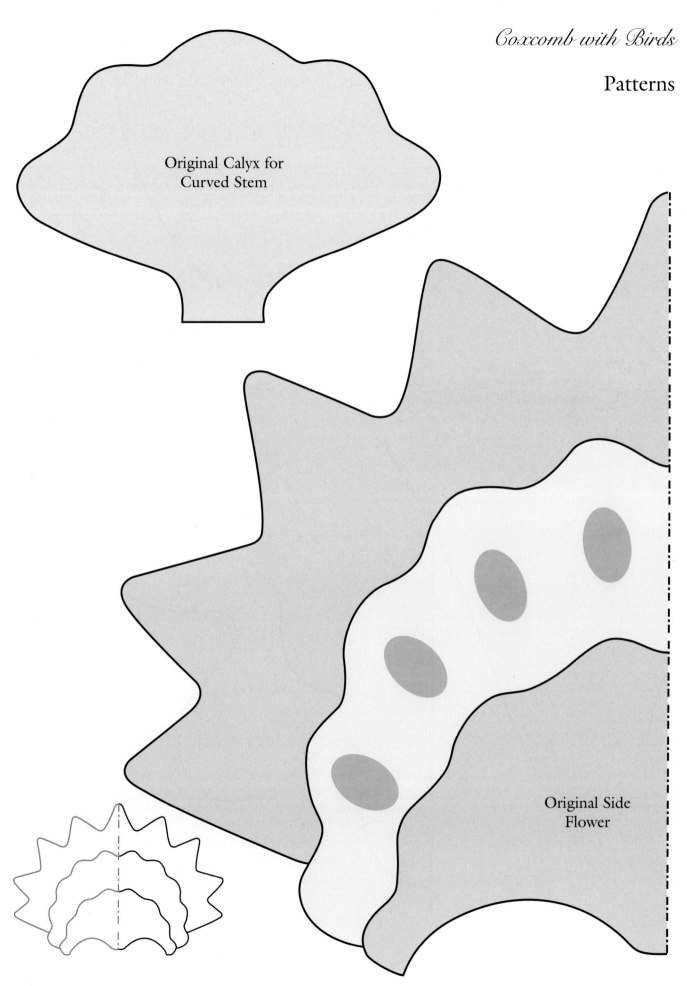

Original Calyx for
Curved Stem

Original Side
Flower

# Patterns

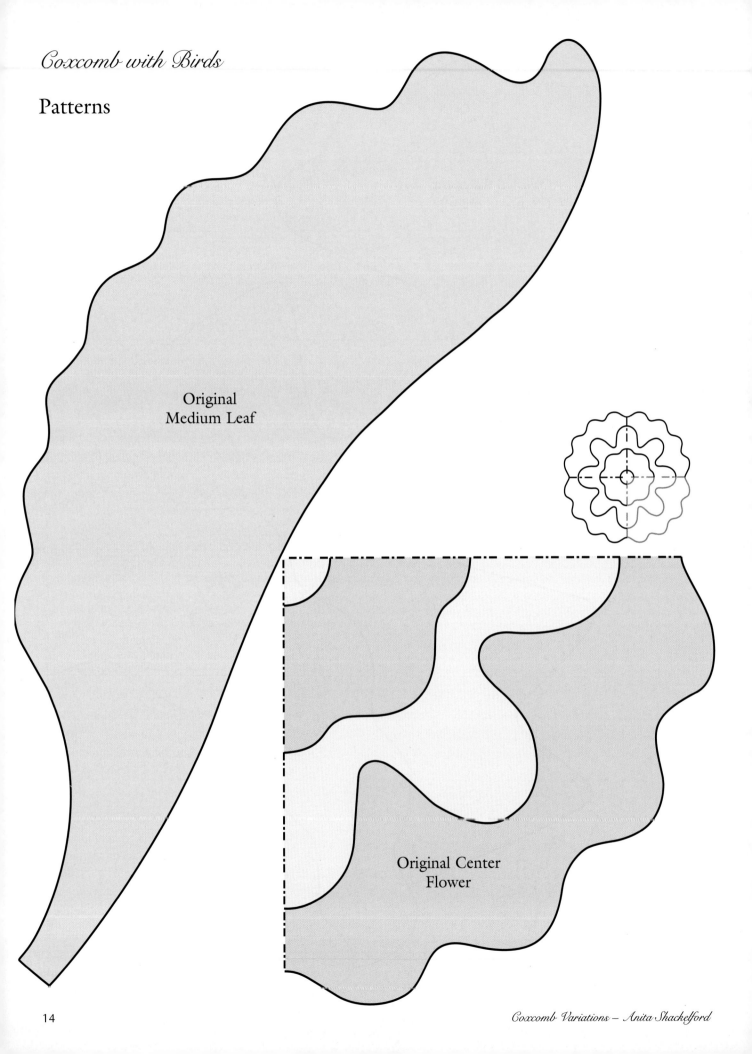

Original
Medium Leaf

Original Center
Flower

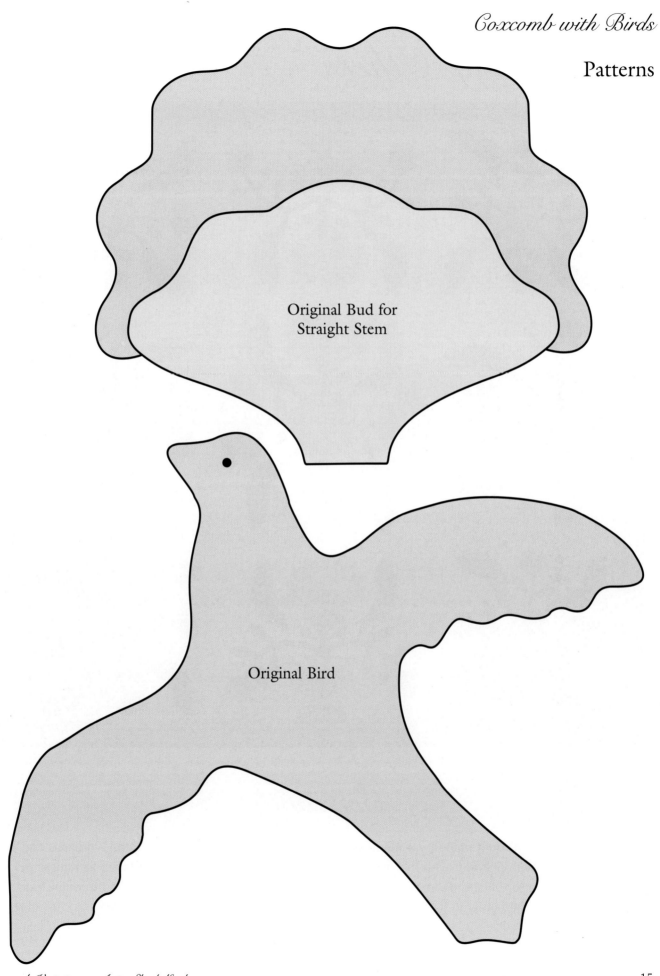

Original Bud for
Straight Stem

Original Bird

# Discovering Others

## Coxcomb

Antique coxcomb quilt made by a member of the Schmidt family in Ripley County, Indiana, and given to Elizabeth Schmidt who married John Westrup in 1863. The quilt was taken to Kansas in 1870 and then to Oklahoma in 1895. The quilt is well documented and has passed through four generations of the family to its current owner, Mabel Steele of Ponca City, Oklahoma.

Imagine my surprise when Nancy Hornback of Wichita, Kansas, sent me a copy of a coxcomb quilt that had been documented in the Oklahoma Heritage Quilt Project in 1987. It showed a quilt that was almost identical to the one that I own. The flower templates and the layout are exactly the same, but the Oklahoma quilt does not include birds. The quilt was made with red, green, and pink fabrics, which would be typical of its Indiana origins. Also note that the quiltmaker used green in the center of the large flower instead of repeating the red of the base petals.

Soon after, another photo arrived from Terry Thompson in Lawrence, Kansas. This one was of a crib quilt in the collection of the Abby Aldrich Rockefeller Folk Art Center, Williamsburg, Virginia. The small quilt consists of only the center coxcomb design, made in red, green, and pink, with six birds circling the floral medallion. This quilt was reportedly made in the same Indiana county as the Schmidt quilt.

All who have seen the photos of these three early quilts feel that there must be some connection, either in family or in community, among their makers.

*Crib Quilt*

45⅛" x 35⅛" Attributed to Alma Richter,
possibly Sunman, Ripley County, Indiana, c.1854.
Collection of the Colonial Williamsburg Foundation, #1985.609.1
Photo courtesy of Colonial Williamsburg Foundation

# The Challenge: Coxcomb Variations

When the reproduction quilt was shown, people found the coxcomb design exciting and unusual and asked if I would share the pattern with them. I issued a challenge to friends to use the same templates, but to create quilts which would be different in color, layout, or interpretation of the pattern.

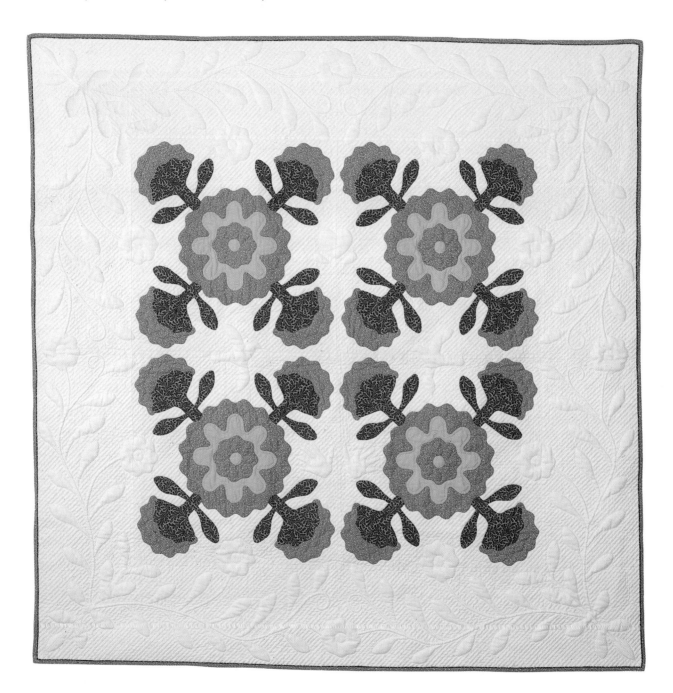

## Sweetheart Rose

Hand appliquéd and hand quilted by the author, 1996

# Sweetheart Rose

This four-block baby quilt uses the large flower, small leaves, and buds from the original quilt, recombined to create a new design. The appliquéd blocks were set directly together and framed with a trapunto flower and vine border. The trapunto leaves are the original size, while the flowers and birds were reduced slightly to fit the space. Additional quilting designs include a heart motif and baby hands, also done in padded trapunto. The background is quilted in parallel lines ¼" apart and the edge is finished with a piped binding.

*Artist's statement –*

This traditional looking design was the first variation that I developed using just a few of the templates. Only the arrangement of the appliqué was changed; the templates are the original size. When I was working on the quilt, I was happy to see that several of the smaller motifs would work as well for the quilting designs as they did for appliqué. I have always felt that repeating an appliqué motif as a background quilting design helps to visually tie together these two areas of a quilt. This special quilt was made for my granddaughter, Amber. The Rose of Sharon-style block would be beautiful for any size quilt.

| Quilt size | 51" x 51" |
|---|---|
| Blocks | 17" |
| Borders | 8" |

## Yardage

1 yd. Pink print (flowers)
⅔ yd. Green print (leaves)
¼ yd. Yellow solid (accent color)
3 yds. Ivory (background)

# Distinctive Design Elements

Trapunto motifs, new arrangement & colors of flowers

## Quilting Design

The flower and leaf appliqué motifs are repeated as trapunto quilting designs. Parallel line quilting fills the background.

Patterns

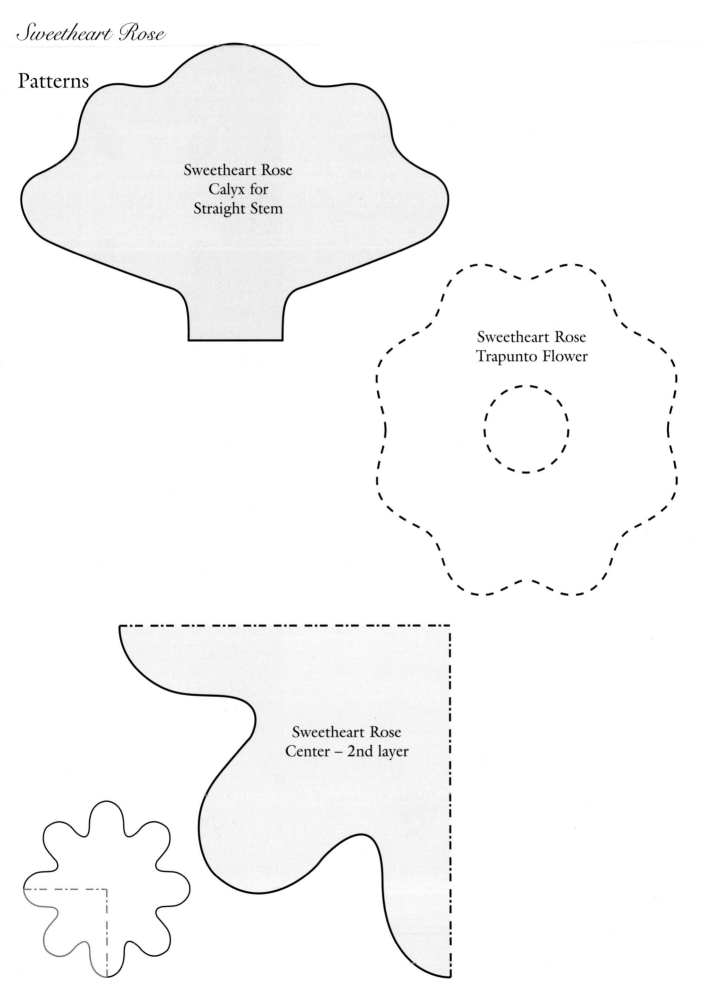

Sweetheart Rose
Calyx for
Straight Stem

Sweetheart Rose
Trapunto Flower

Sweetheart Rose
Center – 2nd layer

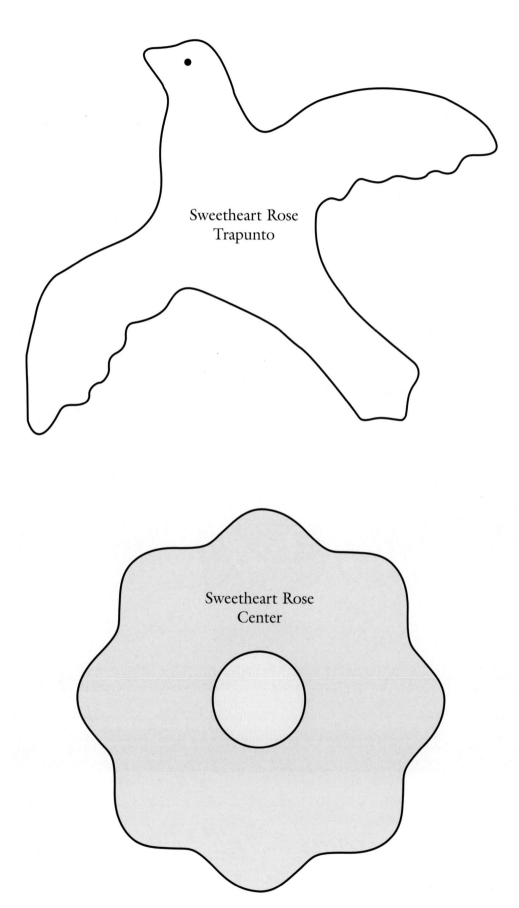

Sweetheart Rose
Trapunto

Sweetheart Rose
Center

# Coxcomb *Variations*

## Coxcomb: Full Bloom

Machine appliquéd and hand quilted by the author, 1997

# Coxcomb: Full Bloom

This wall quilt shows the large spiky coxcomb flowers set in a traditional triple blossom arrangement. The templates are the originals with the exception of a slight change in the large leaf to help it drape more gracefully from the vase. The triple flower motif is an effective way to change a rectangular design into one that fills a square block more completely.

The colors chosen are similar to the original quilt, but they have been placed on a subtle striped background fabric instead of muslin for added color and visual texture. The machine appliqué uses both blanket and satin stitches, in matching and contrasting colors.

A triple strip border with butted corners complements the folk art look of the piece. The edges are finished with a bias binding in a contrasting color.

*Artist's statement –*
The symmetrical arrangement of three flowers in a vase is often found in nineteenth-century appliqué and I felt that these motifs would work well in this arrangement. I love the bold look of these large spiky flowers and the sense that proportion is not very important in folk art design.

| | |
|---|---|
| Block | 35" x 35" |
| Borders | 2", 3", and 3" |

Use the original patterns, pgs. 10–15

## Distinctive Design Elements

Machine appliqué & echo quilting

## Quilting Design

A new stem-and-berry motif was added below the large leaf. Echo quilting with ½" spacing fills the background completely.

## Yardage

1½ yds. Red solid
1½ yds. Green solid
¼ yd. Orange solid
1½ yds. Tan stripe (background)

# Coxcomb *Variations*

*Fire Blossom*

Hand appliquéd and hand quilted by Janet Hamilton, Ashland, Ohio, 2000

# Fire Blossom

Janet Hamilton's wall quilt, which began with the original vase of flowers, shows a design adaptation and new color choices. Slight changes of size and shape were made in the stems and large leaves. The addition of small buds above the central flower and birds in the corners creates a nearly square presentation. Chain stitch embroidery detail adds texture and a line of color to the vase. A double border, in fabrics which repeat the appliqué colors, frames the piece well. The quilt is finished with a piped binding.

*Artist's statement –*
After concentrating on Baltimore-style and highly detailed three-dimensional work, this simpler folk art style was an appealing change. I wanted to create a coxcomb example that would be bold in color and style, eliminating much of the detail that had been my previous focus. I always enjoy working with the study group; this challenge certainly elicited a wide range of styles from one basic pattern.

Change of colors & additional buds

| | |
|---|---|
| Quilt size | 49" x 46" |
| Background block | 36" x 34" |
| Borders | 1¾" and 4" |

## Yardage

⅓ yd. Blue (vase, birds)
½ yd. Green
¼ yd. Rust
⅛ yd. Print
½ yd. Gold
1¼ yd. Blue print (border)
1 yd. Muslin

## Quilting Design

Janet added beautiful lines of quilting within each appliqué motif. Quarter inch echo quilting surrounds the appliqué. The background is filled with a hanging diamonds pattern. Border quilting designs include oak and ivy leaves, birds, and flowers.

Patterns

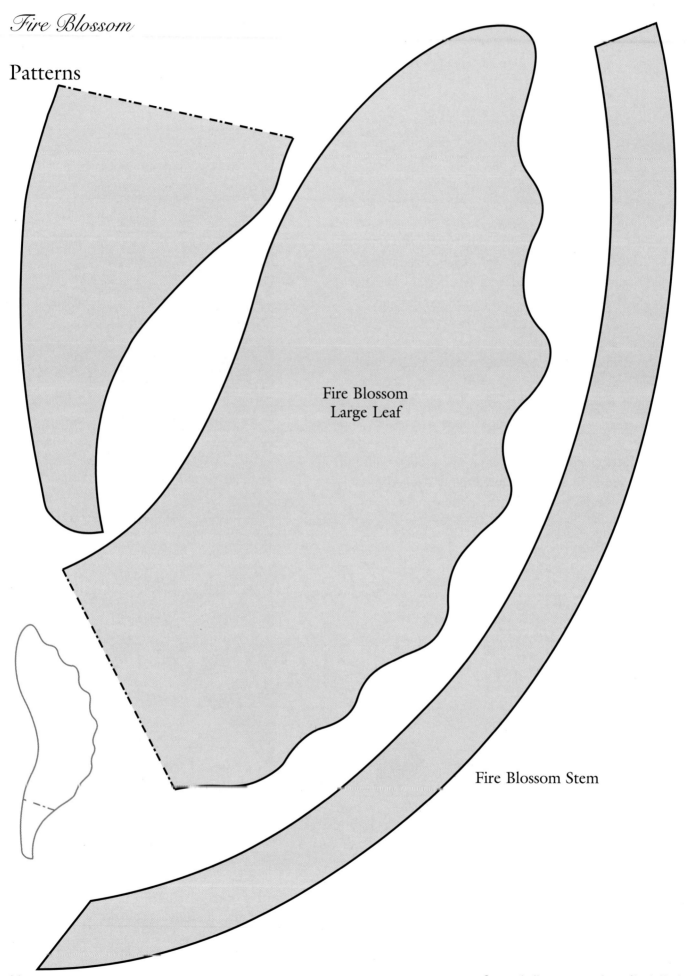

Fire Blossom
Large Leaf

Fire Blossom Stem

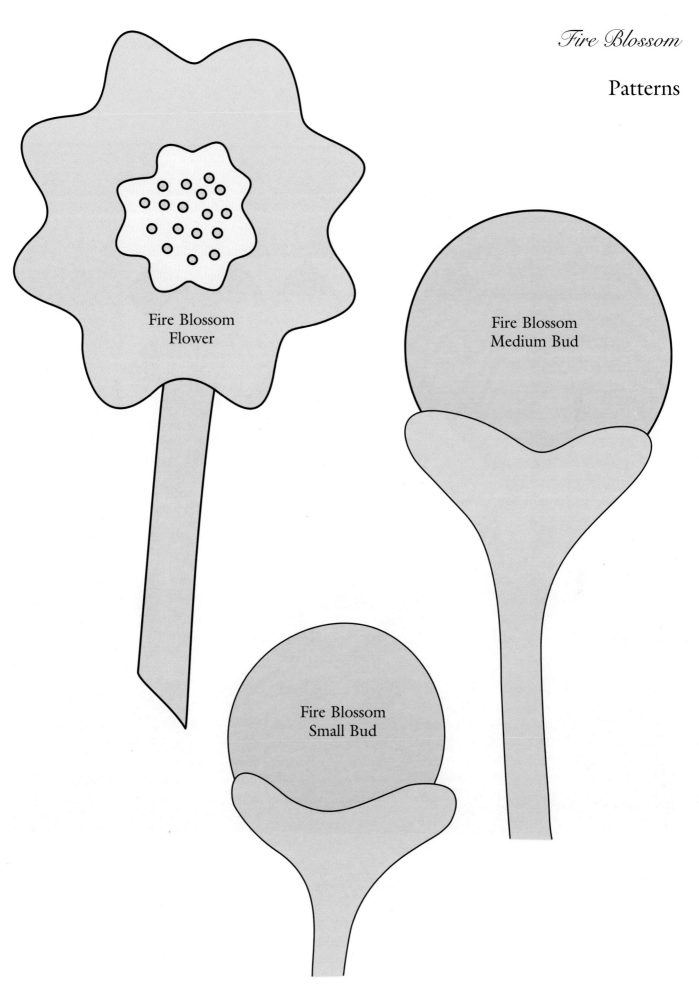

Fire Blossom
Flower

Fire Blossom
Medium Bud

Fire Blossom
Small Bud

# Coxcomb *Variations*

## Coxcomb in the Oakland Museum Tradition
Hand appliquéd and hand quilted by Judy Spence, Powell, Ohio, 1999

# Coxcomb in the Oakland Museum Tradition

Judy Spence's wall quilt was designed with a vase of flowers set on point as a center focus. The medallion arrangement includes setting triangles and a series of pieced and plain borders. Besides the obvious change in layout, Judy reduced the size of the templates, simplified the vase, and added a simple two-part circle motif.

Judy's work, whether pieced or appliqued, often includes many, many fabrics, producing a rich antique scrap look. Working with a collection of reproduction fabrics can give the same look to your quilt. A red binding, which repeats the color of the vase and flowers, adds the finishing touch.

*Artist's statement –*
I have always liked traditional designs and had never used a coxcomb pattern before. I hoped to create a simplified folk-art coxcomb in wall hanging size for my dining room wall, using the Oakland Museum fabrics. I'm happy with the results and feel I accomplished my goal.

| Quilt size | 44" x 44" |
|---|---|

| | |
|---|---|
| Center block | 15½" (finished) |
| Setting triangles | (12⅝" square, cut diagonally) |
| Borders | 2½" half square triangles |
| ¾" | wide red border |
| 6½" | outer border |

## Yardage

Fat quarter for Background block
½ yd. Cream          ½ yd. Brown
⅛ yd. Blue           ¼ yd. Red
1¼ yds. Print border
Other small pieces as desired for appliqué shapes

Upright leaf placement & circle buds

## Quilting Design

Lines of echo quilting surround the vase of flowers. Half feather wreaths add texture to the setting triangles. The triangles of the inner border are quilted by the piece. One inch cross hatch fills the outer border.

# Patterns

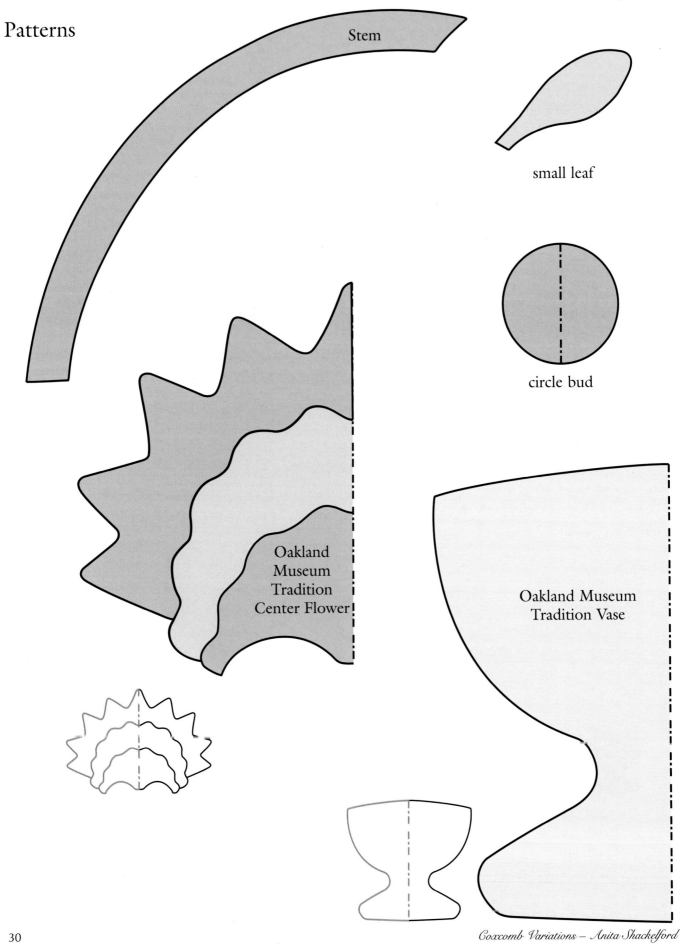

Stem

small leaf

circle bud

Oakland
Museum
Tradition
Center Flower

Oakland Museum
Tradition Vase

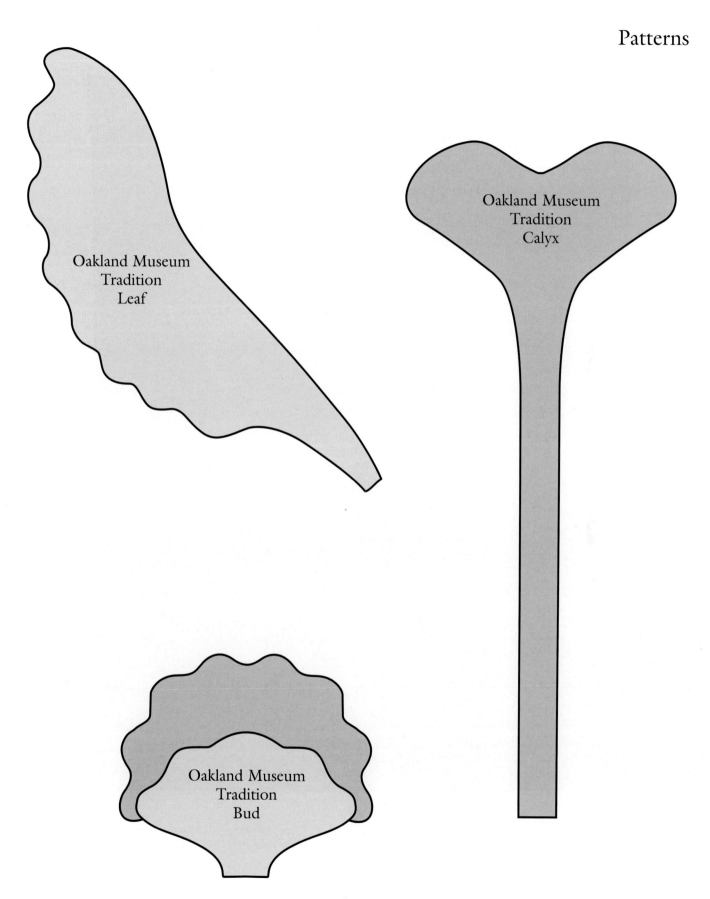

Oakland Museum
Tradition
Leaf

Oakland Museum
Tradition
Calyx

Oakland Museum
Tradition
Bud

# Coxcomb *Variations*

## *Wool Coxcomb*
Machine blanket stitch appliquéd and machine quilted by Erena Rieflin,
Rochester Hills, Michigan, 1998

# Wool Coxcomb

Different fabric choices and a new color palette come together in Erena Rieflin's wall quilt. All of the fabric used in the quilt is wool, which Erena felted by machine washing and drying. The appliqué is done by machine, using a blanket stitch and black perle cotton. The heavy thread adds both detail and texture to the piece.

A more complex arrangement of flowers has produced a design with a vertical presentation. Erena changed the size of two of the leaves, added another layer of petals to the bud, and introduced a new tulip motif to the arrangement. The shape of the vase is simplified, and it has been embellished with additional appliqué details. The one block quilt is framed with a pieced sawtooth border and finished with a simple binding.

*Artist's statement –*
From the moment I saw the pictures of the coxcomb quilts, I wanted to try this pattern. For quite a while I had been thinking of making a wool quilt and so I decided to combine the two. I like the design very much and would like to do it again in cotton.

| | |
|---|---|
| Quilt size | 48" x 62" |
| Center block | 42" x 56" |

3" Half-square triangle border

 ## Yardage

Based on 56" wide wool

| | |
|---|---|
| 2 yds. Black | ½ yd. Red |
| 5" x 8" Dark red | ⅓ yd. Yellow |
| 9" x 20" Pink | ⅓ yd. Green |
| 12" x 24" Blue | |

## Distinctive Design Elements

Modified bud, new tulip, simplified vase & sawtooth border

## Quilting Design

Erena chose simple lines to complement the texture of her heavy wool quilt. The quilting follows the outline of the appliqué designs. Grid quilting fills the background.

Patterns

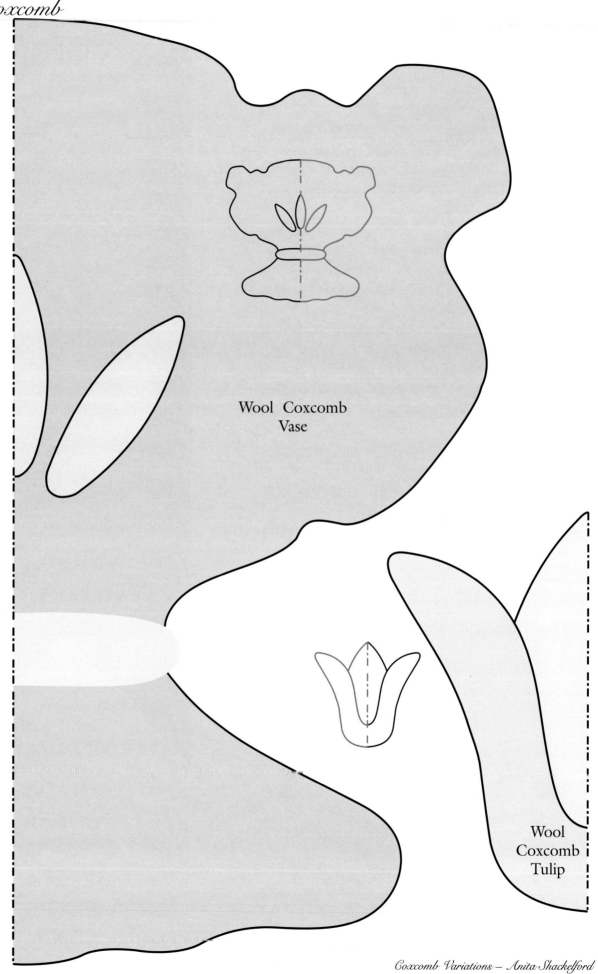

Wool Coxcomb
Vase

Wool
Coxcomb
Tulip

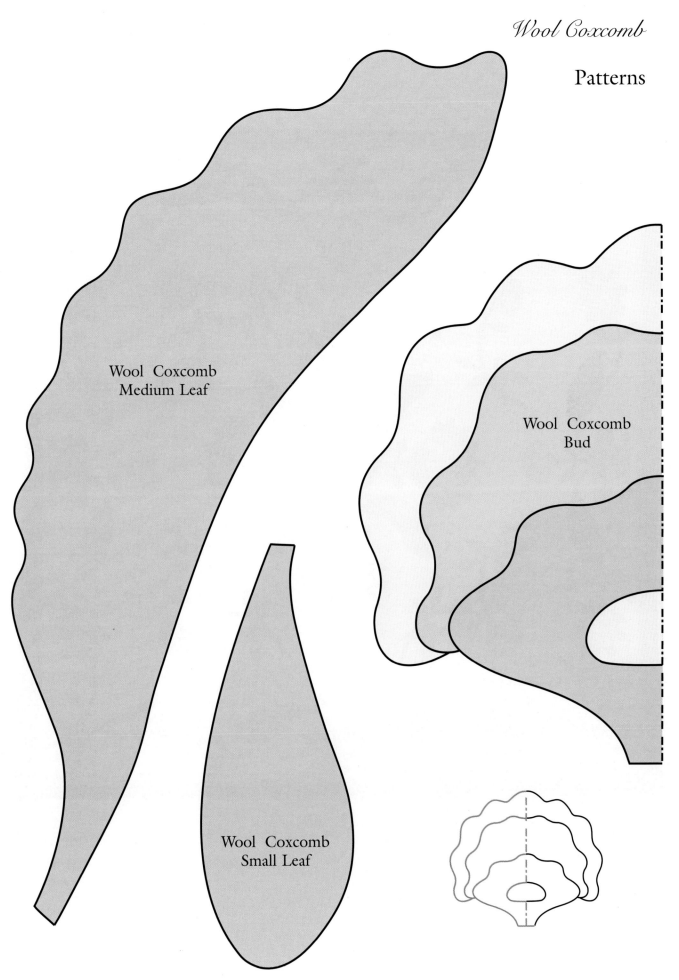

Wool Coxcomb
Medium Leaf

Wool Coxcomb
Bud

Wool Coxcomb
Small Leaf

# Coxcomb *Variations*

## *Bluebirds of Mexico*

Hand appliquéd and hand quilted by Jo Lischynski, Green Springs, Ohio, 1997

# Bluebirds of Mexico

Jo Lischynski's BLUEBIRDS OF MEXICO uses adaptations of both color and layout. She has created a quilt with a very different appearance, with surprisingly little change from the original templates.

Reversing the position of only two large leaves in the center block causes a dramatic change in appearance. With leaves that swirl around the center rather than reaching above the flower, the medallion becomes a block on point. As in Sheila Kennedy's quilt (page 50), the leaves turning in one direction add a feeling of movement to the design. In the new border arrangement, a simplified vase holds the original bud, while small leaves and flowers grow toward the corners. The medium leaf has been altered to drape more gracefully from the vase. Birds and buds made from the original templates combine to fill the interior corners. Double flat piping adds texture and color in the border seams. The quilt is finished with bias binding in a matching color.

*Artist's statement –*
While on vacation in Mexico, I fell in love with the bright colors and the birds in the area. When we returned home and I started this project, all I could envision was the warmth of Puerto Vallarta. I created this piece as an everlasting memory of our holiday there.

| | |
|---|---|
| Quilt size | 78" x 78" |
| Center block | 34" square on point |
| Setting triangle | 24" on short sides |

Borders 13" wide and 3" outer border

 ## Yantal

## Yardage

| | |
|---|---|
| 6 yds. | Muslin (background fabric) |
| 3 yds. | Large print (flowers/border) |
| 1½ yds. | Green solid (leaves, stems) |
| 1 yd. | Yellow solid (flowers, flat border insert) |
| 1 yd. | Red solid (flowers, flat border inserts) |
| ¾ yd. | Blue solid (birds) |

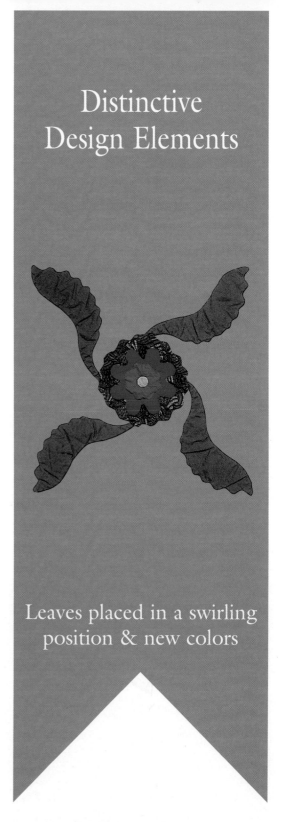

## Distinctive Design Elements

Leaves placed in a swirling position & new colors

## Quilting Design

The background of Jo's quilt is stitched in a double and triple line grid. The contrasting color of thread adds visual texture to the piece.

# Patterns

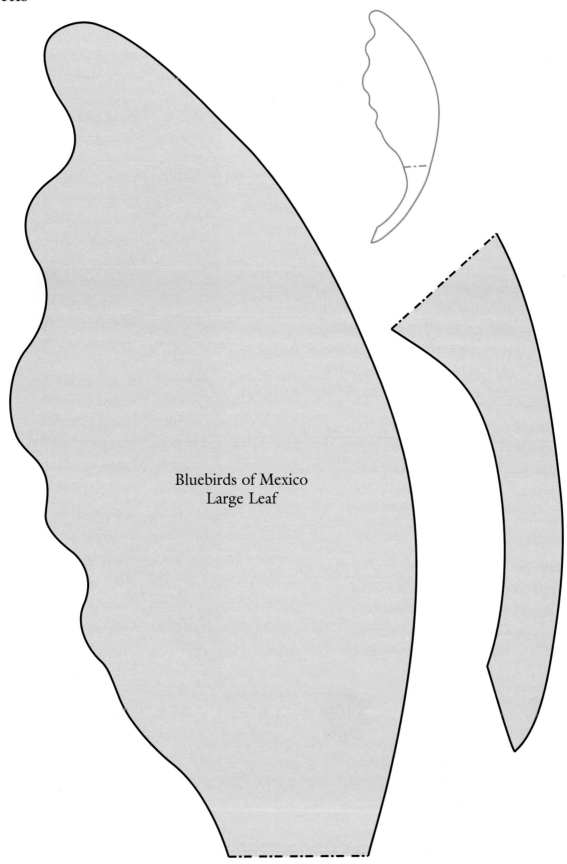

Bluebirds of Mexico
Large Leaf

Bluebirds of Mexico
Calyx

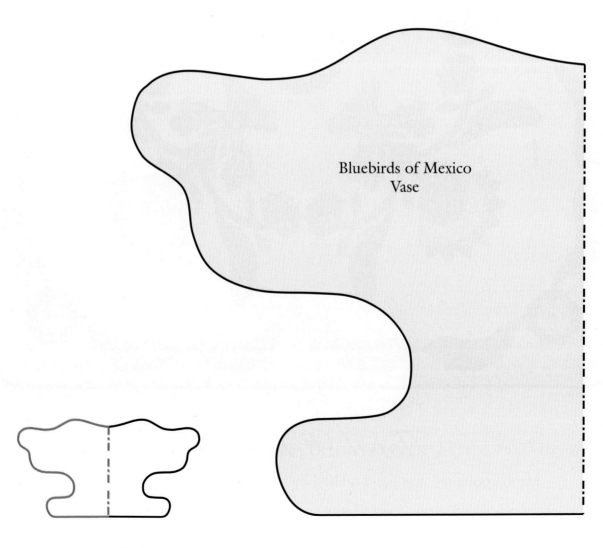

Bluebirds of Mexico
Vase

# Coxcomb *Variations*

## *Floral Renaissance*

Hand appliquéd and hand quilted by Mary Clark, Sylvania, Ohio, 1998

# Floral Renaissance

Mary Clark's variation shows a change in both color and layout. The vase and flower templates are unchanged and repositioned only slightly from the original design. Four large blocks are set together to create a medallion-style center. The long arching stems almost touch as they flow around the center and create a secondary pattern which frames the center design. Mary found that positioning the four dark vases together created a center which seemed slightly heavy. The vase overlay, designed by Sharon Mareska, adds just a touch of light to this part of the design. An additional star-shaped layer in the central flower repeats the pointed crown of the large coxcomb. The large leaves, positioned around the outside edge, produce a swag effect in the border. Curved corners echo the flowing lines of the appliqué design and the edge is finished with a piped binding.

*Artist's statement –*
The simple beauty of this pattern inspired me. My goal was to update an old pattern and make it work for today without losing the flair and elegance of the original. I loved working on this quilt and had a hard time putting it down.

| | |
|---|---|
| Quilt size | 74" x 74" |
| Blocks | 27" square |
| Border | 10" wide |

 ## Yardage

½ yd. Navy     ½ yd. Lt. blue
½ yd. Pink     1 yd. Red
1⅔ yd. Green
5¼ yds. Soft pink (background)

# Distinctive Design Elements

Leaf and bird border
& vase with overlay

## Quilting Design

Mary designed beautiful quilting patterns to add detail to the appliqué motifs in her quilt. Feather plumes are used as accents in several areas. The background quilting includes a meander pattern in the center, while ¾" grid and 1" double line patterns fill the remaining background spaces.

# Patterns

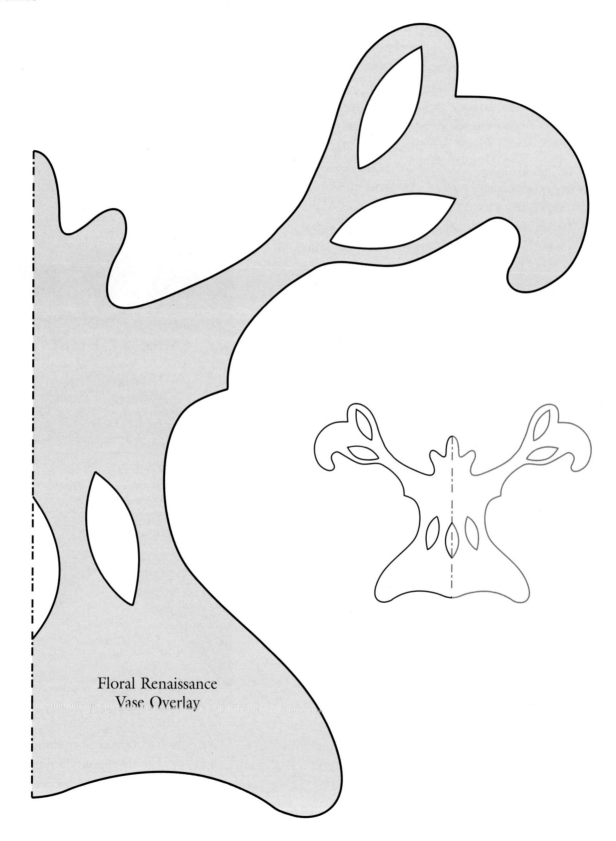

Floral Renaissance
Vase Overlay

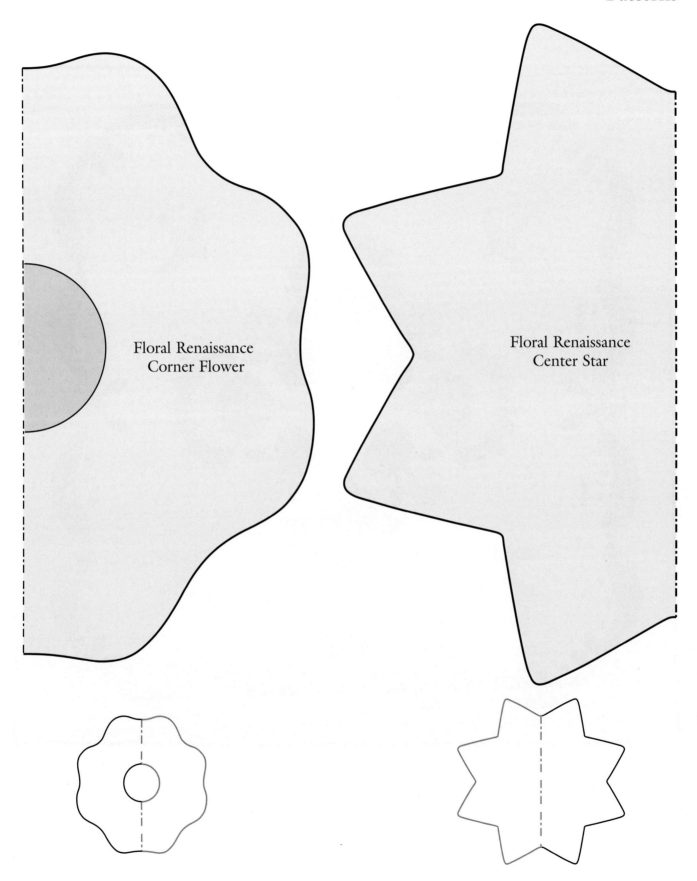

Floral Renaissance
Corner Flower

Floral Renaissance
Center Star

# Coxcomb *Variations*

## Coxcomb Revisited
Machine appliquéd and hand quilted by Sharon Finton, Oakland, Michigan, 1999

# Coxcomb Revisited

Sharon Finton's beautiful medallion arrangement focuses on the original large coxcomb flowers. In place of the large leaves, Sharon used the buds and small flower centers to create an arrangement with slightly more visual weight than the original. The large leaves create a graceful swag-style border that has been embellished with small flowers, leaves, and berries. Birds fill the inner corners. A double-fold bias binding finishes the piece.

*Artist's statement –*

The lovely shapes of this particular coxcomb design are very appealing, easy to work with, and especially suited to straight stitch machine appliqué, as taught by Letty Martin. While I thoroughly enjoy hand appliqué, I wanted to use this machine technique on the quilt to demonstrate that the method can be used to produce a vintage-looking quilt. Because I found the size of the shapes so graphic, I wanted to use as many of them as possible in their original size and thought a center medallion design would provide the focus I was looking for. My goal was to make a warm and cheerful vintage-looking quilt – one that would make me smile.

| | |
|---|---|
| Quilt size | 60" x 60" |
| Blocks | 32" square |

## Yardage

1 yd. each of four fabrics: Red/beige (background)

Fat quarter each of three red fabrics: (4 large and 4 small coxcombs, 48 berries)

Fat quarter each of two yellow fabrics: (4 large coxcombs, 13 small flower centers)

Fat quarter: Double pink (13 small flowers)

1 yd.: Medium green (calyx 4 large coxcombs, 16 leaves)

Fat quarter: Dark green (calyx of 4 small coxcombs, stems of 4 small flowers, 24 small leaves)

Fat quarter: Periwinkle blue (4 birds)

# Distinctive Design Elements

Leaf swag border
& double bud

## Quilting Design

Background quilting patterns include straight lines radiating from the center and a variety of feather designs. Birds are repeated in the border. Appliqué motifs are outline quilted and detailed within. The quilting designs were based on a study of antique quilts and drafted by Sharon to fit the quilt.

# Patterns

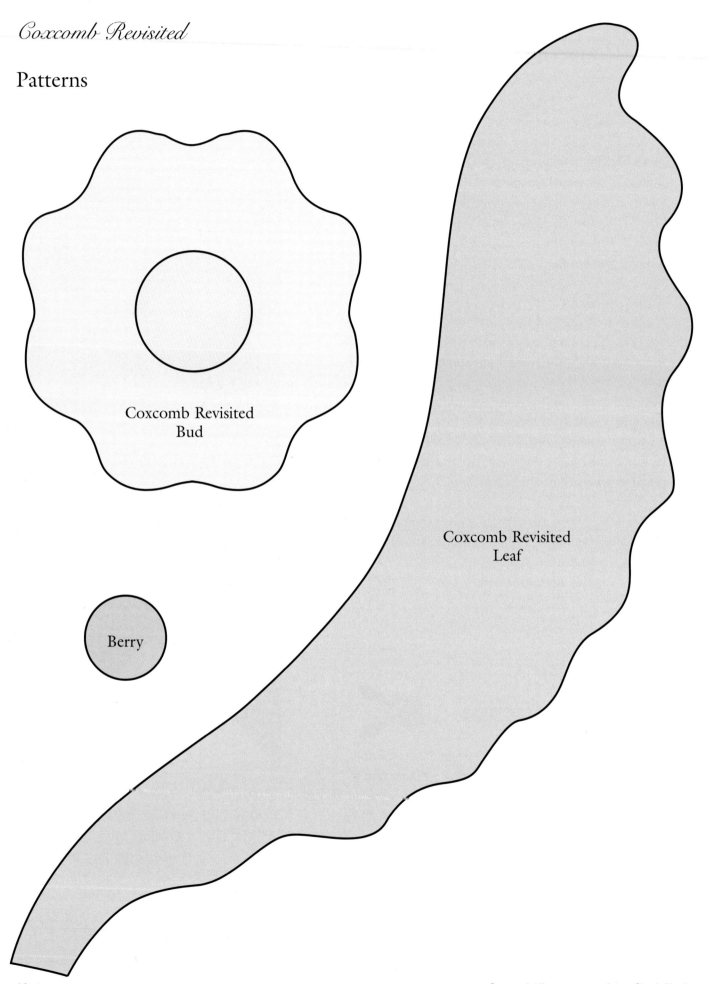

Coxcomb Revisited
Bud

Berry

Coxcomb Revisited
Leaf

# Coxcomb *Variations*

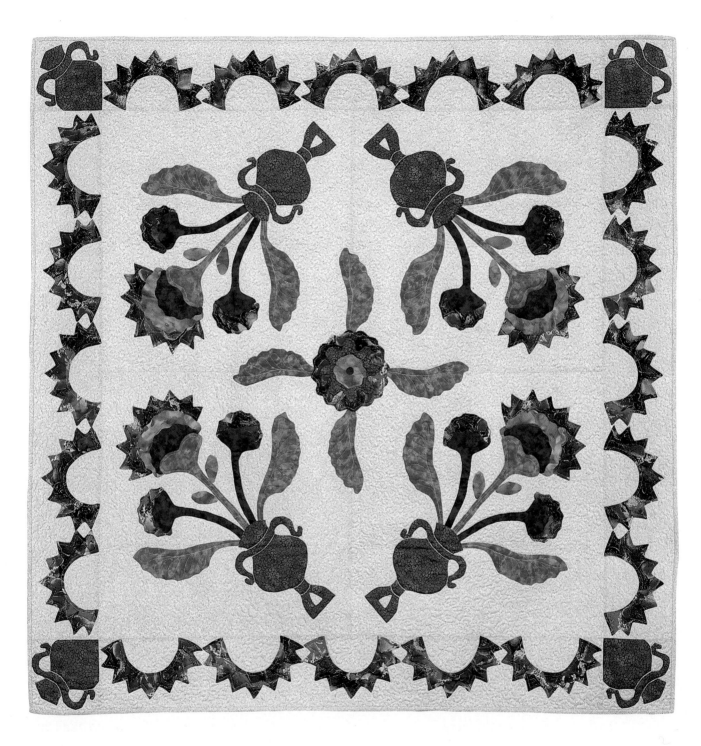

## *Beijing Four Block*

Hand appliquéd and machine quilted by Darlene Garstecki, Oakland, Michigan, 1998

# Beijing Four Block

Darlene Garstecki's BEIJING FOUR BLOCK shows dramatic change in both color and layout. The quilt has a very different look, but was made with surprisingly little variation in the original templates. The center motif uses the large flower and large leaf in a new arrangement. The block design combines a new vase shape with the original coxcomb, leaves, and buds that have been repositioned, but not changed. The crown of the large coxcomb creates a unique swag border along all four sides of the quilt and the vase motif is repeated in the corners. Free-motion embroidery adds a decorative gold band on the teal vases at the handles and the base. The binding fabric matches the background.

*Artist's statement –*

After I made the quilt, I discovered that I had selected colors that were in my vacation pictures from Beijing, China. The walls and ceilings in many of the temples we visited had this color combination and although I did not consciously know it, I am sure this trip influenced the color choices on this quilt. I really enjoyed making the quilt although it was a challenge. I discovered that I have much to learn about appliqué, and this project was a humbling experience.

Quilt size   50" x 50"

Block size        20"
Borders           5½"

## Yardage

| | |
|---|---|
| 2 yds. | Background fabric |
| ½ yd. | Binding |
| ½ yd. | Teal (vases) |
| ⅔ yds. | Coxcomb crowns (4 center coxcombs and border design) |
| ⅓ yd. | Rust (leaves and center stem) |
| Red & gold fat quarters (centers) | |

## Distinctive Design Elements

Crown border, change of colors & new vase

## Quilting Design

Machine quilting outlines each motif and fills the background areas in a random pattern. A modified feather design is used in the large rust leaves. The coxcomb flowers are quilted ¼" from the edge with gold thread. The stems are quilted in a matching rayon thread.

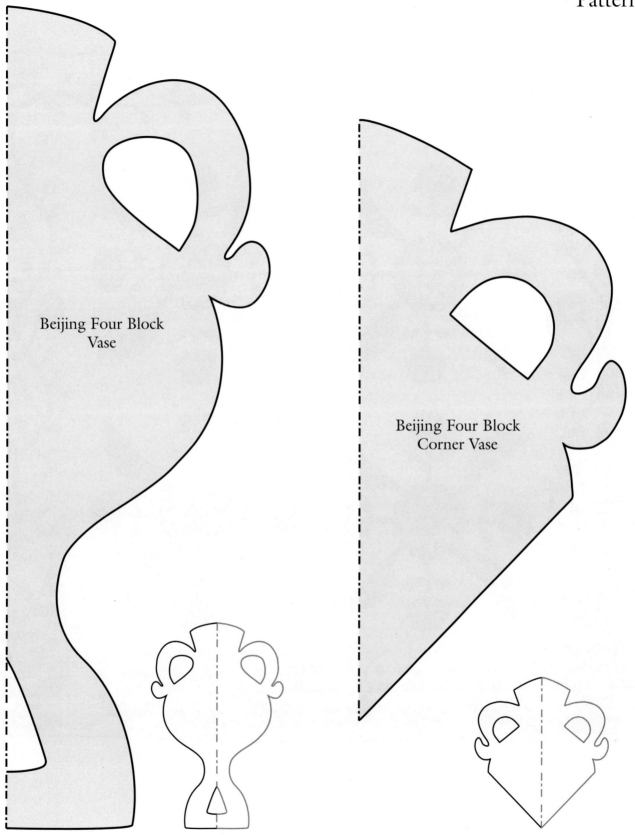

Beijing Four Block
Vase

Beijing Four Block
Corner Vase

# Coxcomb *Variations*

## *Cutters & Coxcombs*

Hand appliquéd and hand quilted by Sheila Kennedy, Bucyrus, Ohio, 2000

# Cutters & Coxcombs

Sheila Kennedy's quilt is a large four-block setting with a wonderful folk art border. The main block design uses the original large center flower, but shows a slight variation in the large leaf which is now scalloped on both sides. The small leaves have been divided into two parts; the two colors effectively change the leaf shape to a bud. In this new arrangement, the large leaves all turn in the same direction, giving somewhat of a Princess Feather feeling to the design. The border is original and includes a running vine with new leaf and flower designs, in a folk art style Sheila finds most appealing. The quilt is finished with a simple bias binding.

*Artist's statement –*
This quilt was a real challenge in several ways. It was my first time working without a complete pattern and my first full size quilt. I was inspired by the simplicity of the quilt layout and by the quilting designs. It was fun to find more quilting patterns in the same style, then to arrange and quilt all of the "cookie cutter" type quilting designs. Just looking at the quilt reminds me of the fun Anita and I had together the day the original quilt was bought at auction. It has been also been fun watching each of the quilts as they have grown and changed.

| | |
|---|---|
| Quilt size | 82" x 82" |
| Blocks | 30" square |
| Borders | 11" |

## Distinctive Design Elements

New folk art border

 ## Yardage

3 yds. Red solid
3 yds. Green solid
½ yd. Orange solid
5 yds. Muslin (background)

## Quilting Design

A line of quilting surrounds each appliqué shape and the background is filled with "cookie cutter" quilting in the style of the original quilt.

# Patterns

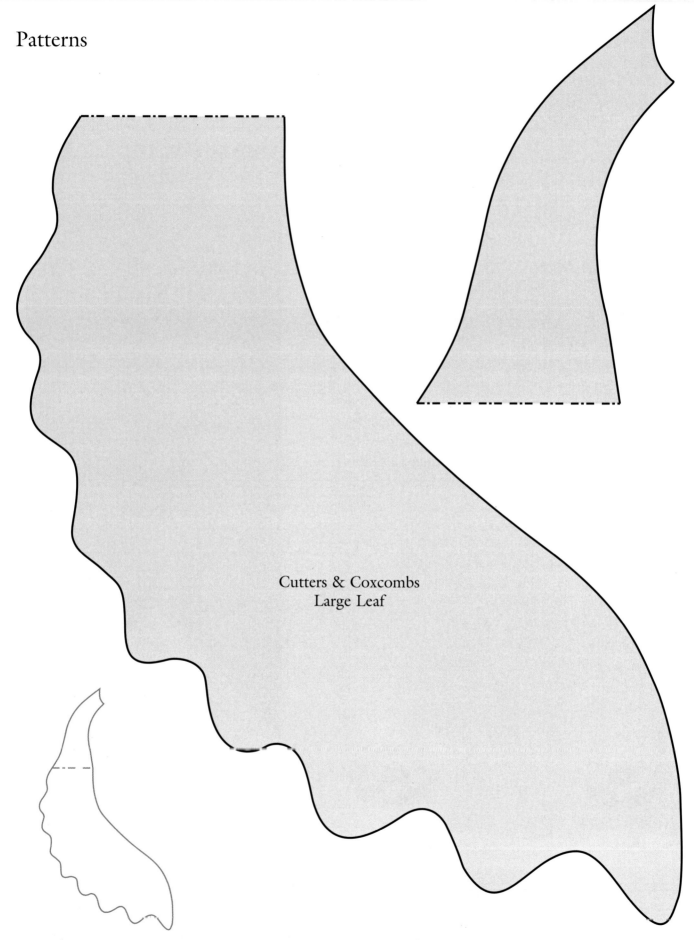

Cutters & Coxcombs
Large Leaf

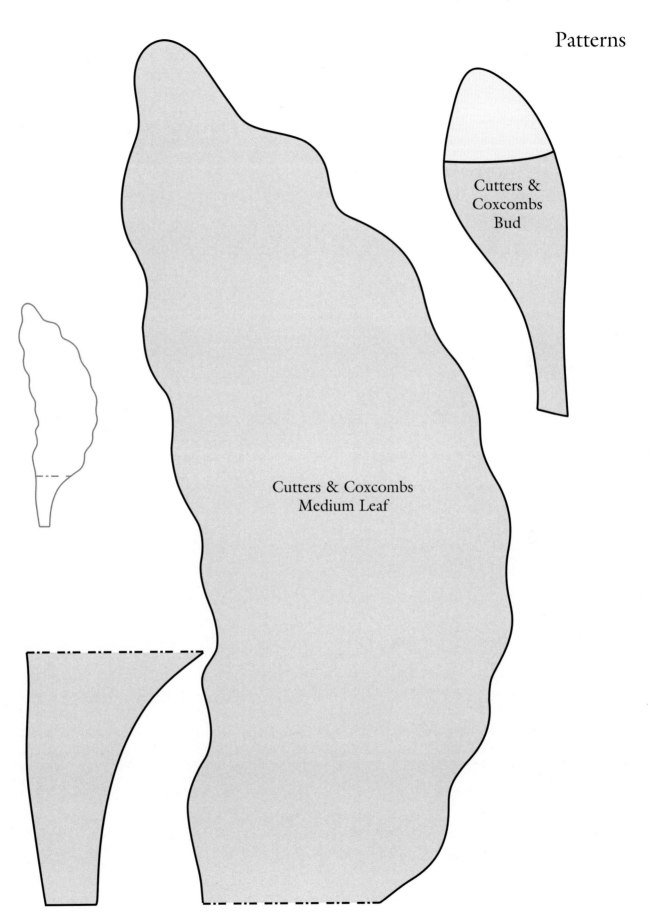

Cutters &
Coxcombs
Bud

Cutters & Coxcombs
Medium Leaf

# Quilting Patterns

# Quilting Patterns

# Coxcomb *Variations*

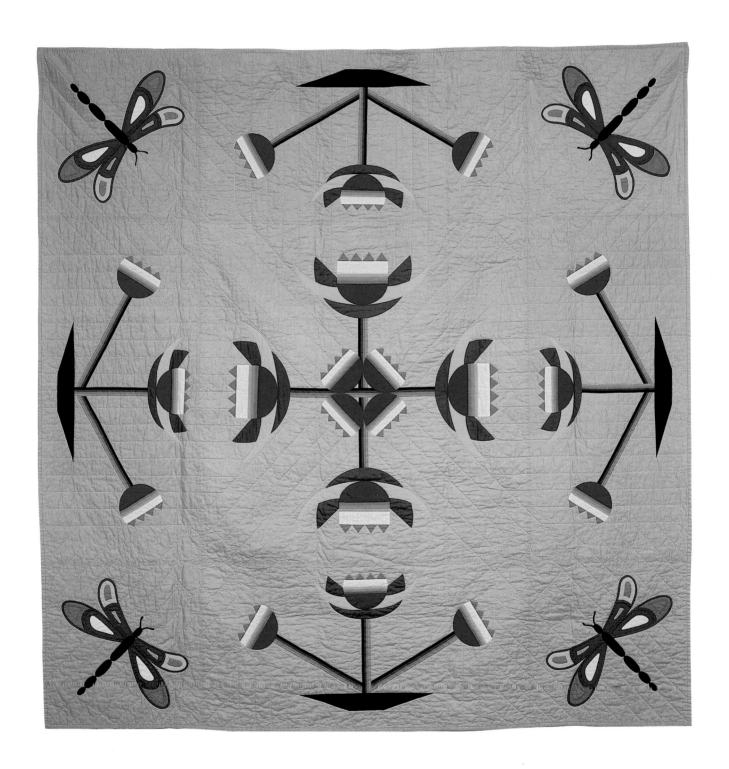

## Desert Flower
Hand appliquéd and machine quilted by Connie St. Clair, Helena, Ohio, 2000

# Desert Flower

Connie St. Clair channels most of her creative talents into garment making, but has joined us in several group quilts and decided to take on this coxcomb challenge as well. She enjoys a bright palette and unusual appliqué motifs in her clothing and her quilt is made with the same flair. If you look closely, you will see that her DESERT FLOWER follows the basic layout of the original quilt. The size and shape of the background blocks and the placement of the appliqué remain the same, but she has used a very innovative interpretation of the vase and flower shapes. The cactus-shaped flowers and beautiful dragonflies in the corner blocks give this quilt a completely different look. The change to a sand-colored background and black, turquoise, lime, and orange for the appliqué shapes support the south-western mood of the piece.

*Artist's statement –*

In my garment making, I enjoy the combination of hand appliqué and machine quilting. I found that the two techniques worked as well together in a large quilt. With this project, I challenged myself to create a more contemporary interpretation of the antique coxcomb quilt, and I am very pleased with the design and the color.

Blocks and border sizes are same as original.

No patterns are provided for this variation.

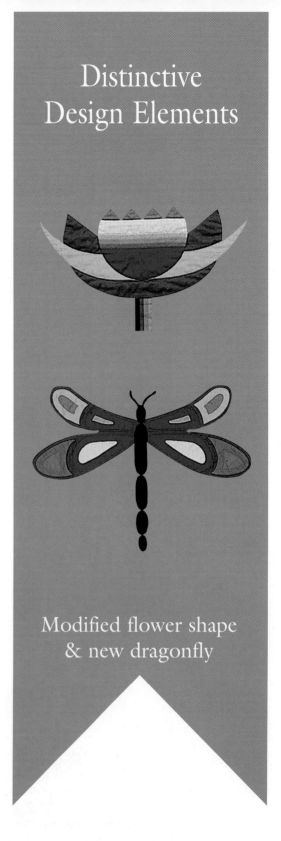

## Distinctive Design Elements

Modified flower shape
& new dragonfly

## Quilting Design

The flower shape is repeated in the quilting. Appliqué motifs are outline quilted, and the background is quilted in horizontal, vertical, and diagonal lines.

  ## Yardage

4½ yds. Tan background
1 yd. Black
¼ - ½ yd. Other colors as desired

# Coxcomb *Variations*

## *Am Eichelgarten 19*
Hand appliquéd and hand quilted by Carol French Grossman,
Rochester Hills, Michigan, 1999

# Am Eichelgarten 19

Thirteen blocks of various sizes make up this sampler of appliqué designs made by Carol Grossman. Although there are recognizable ties to the original coxcomb quilt, Carol has designed a unique and personal piece. She wanted this random sampler of patterns to represent her house and gardens in Wiesbaden, Germany. Although no patterns are included to make this quilt, the following is a list of the block designs and their special meanings.

- Red roses in a blue "Polish Pottery" vase.
- Pink wild geranium in the roses.
- Yellow primrose all through the grass.
- Two brown birds represent my husband and me flying off to Wiesbaden; also brown birds are everywhere.
- Yellow tulips line the length of the terrace in spring.
- Grapes and leaf represent the Rheingau region where we lived; we also had grapes at the side of the house.
- The yard has five huge old apple trees, laden with fruit.
- At the end of the sidewalk is a very tall plum tree with yellow plums.
- At the front steps, a haselhuss (hazelnut) tree drops nuts onto the sidewalk.
- Pine trees are all over the yard.
- Pink and red miniature roses in the terrace garden.
- Eiche (oak/acorn).
- 1998 for the year we lived there.

The borders include Carol's address, plus the oak and ivy that are everywhere. The quilt is bound with a plaid fabric cut on the bias. Some of the designs used in this quilt were taken from *Three-Dimensional Appliqué and Embroidery Embellishment* and *Surface Textures* by the author.

Quilt size        57" x 90"

No patterns are provided for this variation.

## Distinctive Design Elements

Birds in block & new leaf/flower combination

## Quilting Design

Carol's quilt is hand quilted in a broken plaid pattern with single, double, and triple lines spaced 1" apart. The simple lines complement the folk art look of this quilt.

# About the Quiltmakers

*Mary Clark* was taught to quilt at age six by her grandmother. She made a few quilts before she was married, and then made quilts for her children, as they needed them. In 1973, a move to Ohio spurred a greater interest in quilting, and since the time that she discovered appliqué, every spare minute has been spent quilting. Mary lives in Sylvania, Ohio, with her husband Robert. They have three children and seven grandchildren.

*Sharon Finton* has been quilting for 11 years and has completed over 35 quilts. She loves designing her own appliqué and quilting motifs. During the time she lived in Germany, she taught quilting classes and also was invited to lecture and exhibit her work. Sharon and her husband, Doug, now live in Oakland, Michigan, and have one son in college.

*Darlene Garstecki*, a quiltmaker for 12 years, enjoys piecing, appliqué, free-motion embroidery, fusing, and embellishing – whatever method a project needs for completion. She has been a regular contributor to Michigan Quilt Artist's Invitational exhibit and her quilts have won many awards both locally and nationally. Darlene and her husband have three children and a new granddaughter. A retirement move recently took them from Michigan to Hot Springs Village, Arkansas, where Darlene enjoys her quilting and other hobbies of photography, gardening, and golf.

*Carol French Grossman* has been quilting since 1983 and taught quilting from 1984 to 1997. Her husband David's work as a General Motors executive took them to Germany for one year, during which time she made AM EICHELGARTEN 19. Carol and her husband have one married son and currently reside in Rochester Hills, Michigan.

*Janet Hamilton* has been an elementary school teacher for 30 years and a quiltmaker for 11 years. Janet lives in Ashland, Ohio, with her husband Jess. They enjoy art and antiques, and have traveled the world together. Their family includes one daughter, a son and daughter-in-law, and a new granddaughter.

*Sheila Kennedy*, a quiltmaker for 12 years, has a special fondness for folk art appliqué and antique Santas. CUTTERS AND COXCOMBS is the first full-size quilt she has made. Sheila lives in Bucyrus, Ohio, with her husband, Bill, and two sons, Dane and Orry.

*Jo Lischynski* has been a quiltmaker for 20 years, enjoying both pieced and appliquéd quilts. She frequently judges quilt shows in Ohio and for the past several years, has been show coordinator for the National Quilting Association, Inc. For eight years, Jo owned and operated a quilt shop in Green Springs, Ohio, where she and husband, Wally, reside. They have one daughter and son-in-law, and a new grandson.

*Erena Rieflin* was born in Germany and came to the United States in 1966. At that time, she did not know what a quilt was. A picture of a Log Cabin quilt in a magazine was the inspiration for her first quilt, made in 1975. She started to appliqué in 1985 and likes both piecing and appliqué. Erena and her husband, Folker, live in Rochester Hills, Michigan. They have two grown children and enjoy cross-country skiing and bicycle touring.

*Connie St. Clair* has been sewing for more than 30 years and began concentrating on quilted clothing in the early 1990s. Many of her garments include appliqué, with color and design which ranges from subdued to extreme. Her wearables have been published in *Sew News* magazine and have won many awards. Connie lives in Helena, Ohio, with her husband, Larry.

*Judy Spence* works as an independent sales representative for P&B Textiles. She chose the Oakland Museum line of fabric to make her coxcomb quilt as a sample to show at quilt market. She has been quilting for 15 years and a sales representative visiting quilt shops full time for six years – like a kid in a candy store! She is inspired by wonderful quilt shops and motivated by their creative owners. Appliqué has become a real love because it is easy to carry on the road. Judy lives in Powell, Ohio, with her husband, Brent.

## The Author

*Anita Shackelford* has always been in love with nineteenth century appliqué and enjoys drawing inspiration from it to develop new designs. She has been a quiltmaker since 1967 and began teaching in 1980. Over the past 10 years, she has traveled extensively, teaching and lecturing for shops, guilds, and quilting conferences.

Her quilts have been exhibited in shows across the United States and in Australia, winning awards, including 12 for Best of Show and many for workmanship. Two of her quilts have received the Mary Krickbaum Award for best hand quilting at National Quilting Association shows. Her quilts have been published in *American Quilter, American Patchwork & Quilting, Better Homes & Gardens Fashion Ideas, McCall's Quilting, Quilter's Newsletter Magazine, Quilting Today, Quilting International, Quilt Craft, Traditional Quilter, Patchwork Quilt Tsushin, Americana Magazine,* and *Award Winning Quilts and Their Makers Vol. I.*

Anita is the author of *Three-Dimensional Appliqué and Embroidery Embellishment: Techniques For Today's Album Quilt; Anita Shackelford: Surface Textures;* and *Appliqué with Folded Cutwork,* all published by American Quilter's Society. She is also designer of RucheMark ruching guides and the Infinite Feathers quilting design template.

She is a member of the National Quilting Association (NQA) and served for four years on the Board of Directors as membership chairman. She is a member of the American Quilter's Society, the American Quilt Study Group, The Appliqué Society, and Baltimore Appliqué Society. She is a quilt judge, certified by NQA, qualified to judge master quilts, and currently is one of the instructors for NQA's Quilt Judging Seminar.

Anita lives in Bucyrus, Ohio, with her husband Richard. Their family also includes two daughters, Jennifer and Elisa, son-in-law Scott, and two grandchildren, Amber and Brandon.

This is only a small selection of the books available from the American Quilter's Society. AQS books are known worldwide for timely topics, clear writing, beautiful color photos, and accurate illustrations and patterns. These books are available from your local bookseller, quilt shop or public library.

#5234      $22.95

#4829      $24.95

#3788      $24.95

#5175      $24.95

#4833      $14.95

#3789      $16.95

#5012      $22.95

#4898      $16.95

#5338      $21.95

# Look for these books nationally or call
# 1-800-626-5420